Stones in the Road

CUZCO *1981*

Stones in the Road
Photographs of Peru

NUBAR ALEXANIAN

Poem by José Maria Arguédas

CORNERHOUSE
PUBLICATIONS

First published in 1991 by
Cornerhouse Publications
70 Oxford Street
Manchester, M1 5NH
061 228 7621

All rights reserved. No part of this publication may be reproduced or transmitted in any form or by any means, electronic or mechanical, including photocopying, recording or any information storage and retrieval system, without permission from the publishers.

The right of Nubar Alexanian to be identified as author of this work has been asserted by him in accordance with the Copyright, Designs and Patents Act 1988.

© Nubar Alexanian and Cornerhouse Publications

ISBN 0948797 47 9

Design by Ronn Campisi
Printed by Balding and Mansell

For Rebecca and Abby Rose

Photographer's Notes

"Living in this country is like living with stones in the road!" my friend shouted as we made our way from the airport into Lima. He was frustrated by the many obstacles of daily life in Peru, the endless meetings, approvals and paperwork necessary to accomplish even the smallest of tasks. The next day we were on our way north out of the city when we literally came upon stones in the road. Striking workers had rolled large and small stones out into the street to keep buses and cars from passing, forcing people to support the strike by keeping them from work. We were forced to turn around.

I started to think about the phrase, "stones in the road," as the title for my book on Peru. When I mentioned this, my friend was immediately concerned that no one would understand it. He was concerned not for me, but for himself, for Peruvians. It was a good point. The world doesn't know or understand much about Peru.

In the Andean culture of the highlands, stones are not only obstacles, but offerings as well. Travellers place stones in *apachetas,* sacred places along roads through high mountain passes. They carry stones along their journey, offering them as a tribute to the mountain and a prayer for safe passage. Some *apachetas* can be enormous piles of stones, left by travellers over many years.

Stones In The Road grew on me. It especially reminded me of a photograph I had taken a few years earlier of an Indian woman and her daughter (or granddaughter) walking through the streets of Cuzco. They looked lost, centuries lost, walking in step along a cobblestoned street. In the 16th century, the Spanish forced the Incas to tear down their magnificent stone

Stones in the Road

PHOTOGRAPHER'S NOTES

work in Cuzco, using the stones to build churches and a cathedral, and to pave the streets. Along with melting their gold artifacts down to bullion for shipment to Spain, this left them with few symbols to reflect their own heritage in their own land. Today, though they have little or no identity in the modern world, they fiercely protect what's left of their deep cultural roots. In a sense, they carry their culture with them, like secrets kept alive in a timeless world, as if waiting....waiting for something you and I might never expect or understand.

I've been in love with Peru for a long time, since 1974 when I first visited there. It started out as infatuation, I guess. I was young and had never travelled outside the United States. Peru took hold of me during this first trip and wouldn't let go. I travelled across the entire country with a view camera, taking photographs of Inca ruins and dramatic landscapes. They were beautiful photographs, some of which are included on these pages. But there was so much missing in them. Like most visitors, I too, had walked right past Peru on my way to the rich past of the Incas, not knowing and never asking. And as a photographer I felt unchallenged by the work. Taking beautiful photographs of beautiful things was easy. There was too much "taking" in them. I wanted to go deeper, to know Peru in an intimate and personal way.

Beginning in 1978 and for the next eleven years, Peru became my sacred place to work. I accepted no assignments there and returned as often as possible,

making 9 trips in all. I replaced the view camera with 35mm cameras to be less deliberate and more spontaneous. Other than this, I had no idea or plan of how to work. I simply wandered the country with my cameras.

Most of the photographs in this book come from three places: the mountain village of Chinchero, the old Inca capital of Cuzco and the shanty towns surrounding Lima. I travelled all over the country, from desert to jungle, and through countless mountain villages, but found myself returning to these three places over and over again. I was especially attracted to Chinchero, one of the many villages inhabited by Quechua Indians, descendants of the Incas. Even during my first visit, I had the odd sensation of familiarity, like returning after a long absence.

Situated on a high plain in the Urubamba Valley, the Sacred Valley of the Incas, the physical beauty of Chinchero and the surrounding landscape are breathtaking — like nothing I've ever seen. At this high altitude of 3,000 meters, the land is flat, with small rolling hills and high mountains rising above it.

This high plain and Chinchero's close proximity to Cuzco inspired earlier governments to plan an international airport there, creating enormous pressure from the outside world onto this ancient place. This airport, if built, could dramatically change Chinchero, shifting its centuries-old agrarian economy to a service oriented tourist economy. Fields of barley and potatoes would be paved into a runway, bringing plane-loads of

PHOTOGRAPHER'S NOTES

tourists directly from Europe and the United States. The villagers were afraid. I was horrified!

Chinchero has an Inca ruin which is small compared to others in the valley, so it's not a real draw for tourists. I love this ruin and would sit there for hours reading when I wasn't photographing. Each Sunday I would wake up early and go to sit there, listening to people making their way to the Sunday market from the surrounding communities. The silence of this place is so profound I could hear people coming from very far away, rushing down the mountain paths and talking in their native Quechua, a language that sounds like the wind. All at once, the village square was filled with Quechua Indians trading vegetables, drinking chicha (their native alcoholic drink), or walking to Sunday services in the church which serves the local communities. This was the one time each week when everyone came out of the fields to congregate.

On one particular Sunday in 1981, there was a large meeting of hundreds of villagers in the square. I had never seen such a meeting. I was photographing the entire event, not understanding what was going on since they were speaking Quechua. Suddenly, they all stormed the police station. Just as suddenly, the policeman came out and fired his gun into the air, momentarily dispersing the crowd. Then, to my surprise, the villagers started to throw stones at me. The policeman grabbed me and we ran down to the main road, stopped a truck and rode into Cuzco.

Apparently, someone had stolen the gold chalice from the church the previous Thursday evening. I was the prime suspect, being the only outsider. The policeman assured them it could not have been me since, luckily, I ate dinner with him that night and he saw me go to sleep. The villagers concluded that the policeman and I had conspired to steal the chalice, which of course was not true. Along with the physical danger I had unknowingly placed myself in, I was equally startled to discover how much of an outsider I really was.

I never did find out what really happened. I returned two years later, concerned that they would remember the event, and unhappy to discover that they didn't remember me at all. I went to visit the policeman and found a small group of army troops camped around his station. Apparently, one of the rebel forces challenging the government had killed the policeman, bringing a violent civil war and the outside world closer to Chinchero.

My relationship with Chinchero was complicated. I felt such a strong connection with this place that during each trip, I couldn't wait to get there. But once I arrived, I couldn't wait to leave. It's not that I felt misunderstood. It was worse than that. My feelings for this village were not reciprocated in any way. It took years before I was invited to a wedding or a meal in someone's house.

Then it happened all at once. On the third Sunday in March of 1988, I was invited to four separate

Stones in the Road

PHOTOGRAPHER'S NOTES

weddings. To my surprise, there was intense competition among these four families for my attendance. They walked me to their homes in the village to make certain I could find my way to each wedding reception. One mother even pointed to the hour on my watch to make sure I knew what time to be there. I had become the village wedding photographer.

These were my most exciting and exhausting days in Chinchero. The celebrations continued night and day for two or three days, eating, drinking, dancing and sleeping. After this formidable initiation, whenever I entered the village, women and children would rush down the hill to greet me and men would invite me for beer and chicha.

Chinchero has not changed very much in years, decades and even centuries. There is a constancy to the rhythm of life there that gives it a magical and timeless quality. Back in the United States, or travelling in another part of the world, I could close my eyes at any moment of any day, and imagine what was going on in the village. I am amazed that it's been this way for so long, given the pressure Chinchero has endured from the outside world. Even though most of the Indians have been converted to Christianity, their centuries-old rituals and ceremonies remain a prominent part of their lives. Everything in the world is alive to them: stones, soil, mountains, rain. They make offerings to the spirit who inhabits the mountains before planting their crops or passing along a mountain trail. Chinchero, alive with these spirits, is a magical place, filled with mystery and myth. Mystery and myth......two important ingredients for a culture with any substance and so seemingly absent from my own.

Yes, they are poor. They live a meager agrarian existence in the mountains, farming rugged terrain. And though I did not see much migration from Chinchero itself, poverty, the civil war, drug traffickers, and the restlessness of younger generations, have all contributed to a great migration out of mountain villages like Chinchero into the shanty towns of Lima.

Sadly, this migration appears to be the beginning of the end of their culture. It's almost as if Lima is a negation of everything Andean. From year to year I could see the richness of their past fading in the deserts of Lima. The shock of city life on the coast, along with the enormous task of providing for a family in this foreign environment, make it almost impossible for their past to accompany them into the future. Their heritage is diminished from a living reality into a distant memory, while the future becomes more and more prominent. Eventually, a few families do make it into what can be called middle class status. And naturally their children want the things that bring them further into the modern world. Ironically, this points them in the direction of Miami, which has become an inspirational force and a sought after destination.

In 1983 I befriended a priest who lived in one of the older shanty towns of Lima. Hundreds of families

Stones in the Road

PHOTOGRAPHER'S NOTES

migrate each month from the mountains into shanty towns, living in small shacks with no water, electricity or sanitation. During one of my visits a young woman rushed in to see this priest, carrying her sick child, her eyes pleading for help. The urgency in her face was one I would expect to see in a hospital emergency room. But this was no hospital and there was no doctor present.

She wanted him to perform an "emergency baptism" for her child, which priests were asked to do routinely. This particular child was not very sick, but in Peru, people instinctively fear the worst. A slight fever can be a sign that their child is about to be taken from them and the high infant mortality rate certainly supports their fears. The priest explained that they also feel that God has not blessed their country. When they look at the United States, they see a country that has been blessed. Their own poverty is evidence against them. Not surprisingly, and against such odds, a doctor can only do so much. Besides, concluded the priest, they cannot afford to buy the medicines that a doctor might prescribe.

It's difficult to see another country, or know another people, without leaving something of our own country behind. When this doesn't happen, we tend to see a country for what it is not, rather than for what it is. There is a poem by Robert Frost in which he describes a man peering down into a water-drawn well, trying to see what lies at its bottom. He is continually frustrated by his own reflection in the water's surface, often unable to see past it. But he keeps on looking. To me this poem speaks to one of the primary struggles of being a photographer: looking for truth while encountering one's own reflection.

Peru is more than Inca ruins and dramatic landscapes, more than pictures of Indians wearing colorful costumes. When I look at Peru, I see the soul and spirit of the Andean people threatened and I feel threatened also. Is something dying in Peru that is also dying in the rest of the world and going unnoticed? The majority of people in Peru are Indians living much as they have for centuries. They have lived their lives through generations of change, from the Spanish conquistadors to the confusion of civil war and drug traffickers. They are struggling to survive and hold on to what is sacred, while the magic and mystery of their lives and their land is being threatened by poverty and hopelessness. What will their loss mean for the rest of us?

José María Arguedas, the son of a traveling judge, was born in Andahuaylas, Peru at an altitude of three thousand meters. He was reared in the highlands where his first world was the world of the Indians and Quechua his first language. He often wrote his novels and poems in Quechua first, which he then translated into Spanish. My friend who unwittingly offered the title, Stones in the Road, suggested this poem, which creates a powerful tension between the old and the modern, the Indigenous and the Spanish, and is at the same time a hymn to love and an innvocation to harmony.

To the Attention of Certain Doctors

José María Arguedas
1911-1969
(Translated from *harawi-haylli*)

TO CARLOS CUETO FERNANDINI AND JOHN V. MURRA

They say that we know nothing anymore, that we're what's backwards, that they'll
    change our head for a better one.
They say that our heart, too, is obsolete, that it's burdened with fear and with crying,
    like the heart of the lark, like the huge bull that's slaughtered; they say that's
    why it's impertinent;
They say some doctors say this about us; doctors who bear offspring on this same
    land, who grow fat here or turn yellow.
Well then, let them talk; let them chatter if that's what they want.
What is the stuff my brains are made of? What is the flesh of my heart made of?
Rivers run bellowing in the night. Gold and the night, silver and the terrible night
    forging the rocks, the walls of the chasm where the river sounds; my mind, my
    heart, my fingers are made of that rock.
What is there on the shore of those rivers unknown to you, doctor?
Get out your telescope, your best glasses. Look, if you can.
Five hundred flowers from different potatoes grow on the ledges of those chasms
    that your eyes can't see, on the earth where night is mixed with gold, day with
    silver. Those five hundred flowers are my brains, my flesh.
Why has the sun stood still for a moment, why has its shadow disappeared from
    everywhere, doctor?
Start your helicopter and come up here, if you can make it. The feathers of the
    condors, of the small birds are a rainbow and it's radiant.
The colors of the hundred *quinua* flowers that I planted on the peak are burning in
    the sunlight; the black wing of the condor, of the small birds, are flowers.
It's noon; I'm next to the sacred mountains; magnificent, in yellow flashes, in red
    blotches, the snow casts its light to heaven.

On this cold earth I sow *quinua* of a hundred colors, of a hundred kinds, of potent
    seed. The hundred colors are also my soul, my untiring eyes.

Stones in the Road

Fluttering with love, I will extract from your brains the imbecile stones that have
    crushed you.
The sound of the precipice no one reaches, the light of the reddish snow flashing,
    astonishing, on the peak;
into your blood, in the apple of your eye I will spill the precious sap of thousands of
    herbs, of thousands of roots that think and know.
The heartbeat of myriads of worms that keep earth and light; the clamor of flying
    insects, I will show them to you, my brother, I will help you to understand
    them;
the tears of the singing birds, their breast whose caress is like dawn, I will help you
    to feel them and hear them.
What I know, what I suffer, what I delight in the delight of the world was made by
    no difficult machine.
On this earth, from the bone-shattering snow to the fire of the canyons, facing
    heaven, with his will and my strength we did all this.
Don't run away from me, doctor, come closer! Look at me, recognize me. How
    long must I wait for you?

Come closer to me; lift me into the cabin of your helicopter. I will treat you to essences
    of a thousand different saps;
the life of a thousand plants I have cultivated over centuries, from the foot of the
    snowy peaks to the forests where the wild bears have their dens.
I will cure the fatigue that clouds you at times like a lead bullet; I will gladden you
    with the light of the hundred *quinua* flowers, with the vision of their dance in
    the blowing wind; with the small heart of the lark where the world's image is
    reflected; I will refresh you with the clear water that sings, that I draw from
    the walls of the chasms that cool our creatures with their shade.
Will I work for centuries of years and months for someone who's a stranger to me
    and to whom I'm a stranger to cut off my head with a small machine?

No, little brother of mine. Don't help to sharpen that machine against me; come
    closer, let me get to know you; look carefully at my face, my veins; the wind
    that blows from my land to yours is the same wind; we breathe the same
    wind; the land where you count your machines, your books and your flowers,
    descends from mine, bettered, tamed.
Let them sharpen knives, let them make the whips roar; let them mould clay to
    deform our faces; let them do all that.
We don't fear death; for centuries we have choked death with our blood, we have
    made it dance on known and unknown roads.
We know that they want to disfigure our faces with clay; to show us like that,
    disfigured, to our children so that they will kill us.

We're not sure what will happen. Let death walk towards us; let those men we don't
    know come to meet us. We will wait for them on our guard; we are children
    of the father of all the rivers, of the father of all the mountains. Is the world
    not worth anything anymore, little brother of mine, doctor?
Don't answer that it is worth nothing. Greater than my strength, over thousands of
    years perfected; than the muscles of my neck over thousands of months, over
    thousands of years strengthened, is life, eternal life of mine, the world
    without rest, creating without fatigue; giving birth and producing like time,
    with no end and no beginning.

March, 1966   Translated from the Spanish by Christine Graves

José María Arguedas, hijo de un abogado que actuó de juez y fiscal en diversos pueblos del Perú, nació en Andahuaylas, capital de la provincia del mismo nombre, del Departamento de Apurimac. Se crió entre indios en la sierra andina. Su primera lengua fue el quechua, en el que escribía muchas veces los primeros borradores de sus novelas y poesías, para traducirlos después al castellano. Un amigo mío, al mencionar con otro propósito el título "Piedras en la carretera", también trajo mi atención sobre este poema, el cual crea una fuerte tensión entre lo antiuo y lo moderno, lo indio y lo español, siendo a la vez un himno al amor y una invocación a la armonía.

Llamado a Algunos Doctores

José María Arguedas
1911-1969
(Traduccion del *harawi-haylli*)

A CARLOS CUET FERNANDINI Y JOHN V. MURRA

Dicen que ya no sabemos nada, que somos el atraso, que nos han de cambiar la cabeza por otra mejor.
Dicen que nuestro corazón tampoco conviene a los tiempos, que está lleno de temores, de lágrimas, como el de la calandria, como el de un toro grande al que se degüella; que por eso es impertinente;
Dicen que algunos doctores afirman eso de nosotros; doctores que se reproducen en nuestra misma tierra, que aqui engordan o que se vuelven amarillos.
Que estén hablando, pues; que estén cotorreando si eso les gusta.
¿De qué están hechos mis sesos? ¿De qué está hecha la carne de mi corazón?
Los rios corren bramando en la profundidad. El oro y la noche, la plata y la noche temible forman las rocas, las paredes de los abismos en que el rio no suena; de esa roca están hechos mi mente, me corazón, mis dedos.
¿Qué hay al la orilla de esos rios que tú no conoces, doctor?
Saca tu largavista, tus mejores anteojos. Mira, si puedes.
Quinientas flores de papas distintas crecen en los balcones de los abismos que tus ojos no alcanzan, sobre la tierra en que la noche y el oro, la plata y el dia se mezclan. Esas quinientas flores son mis sesos, mi carne.
¿Por qué se ha detenido un instante el sol, por qué ha desaparecido la sombra en todas partes, doctor?
Pon en marcha tu helicóptero y sube aqui, si puedes. Las plumas de los cóndores, de los pequeños pajaros se han convertido en arco iris y alumbran.
Las cien flores de la quinua que sembré en las cumbres hierven al sol en colores; en flor se han convertido la negra ala del cóndor y de las aves pequeñas.
Es el mediodia; estoy junto a las montañas sagradas; la gran nieve con lampos amarillos, con manchas rojizas, lanza su luz a los cielos.

En esta fria tierra siembro quinua de cien colores, de cien clases, de semilla poderosa. Los cien colores son también mi alma, mis infatigables ojos.

Yo, aleteando amor, sacaré de tus sesos las piedras idiotas que te han hundido.
El sonido de los precipicios que nadie alcanza, la luz de la nieve rojiza que, espan-
          tando, brilla en las cumbres;
el jugo feliz de millares de yerbas, de millares de raices que piensan y saben,
          derramaré en tu sangre, en la niña de tus ojos.
El latido de miriadas de gusanos que guardan tierra y luz; el vocerio de los insectos
          voladores, te los enseñaré, hermano, haré que los entiendas;
Las lágrimas de las aves que cantan, su pecho que acaricia igual que la aurora, haré
          que las sientas y oigas.
Ninguna máquina dificil hizo lo que sé, lo que sufro, lo que del gozardel mundo
          gozo.
Sobre la tierra, desde la nieve que rompe los huesos hasta el fuego de las quebra-
          das, delante del cielo, con su voluntad y con mis fuerzas hicimos todo esto.
¡No huyasde mi, doctor, acércate! Mirame bien, reconóceme ¿Hasta cuando he de
          esperarte?

Acércate a mi; levántame hasta la cabina de tu helicóptero. Yo te invitaré el licor de
          mil savias diferentes;
la vida de mil plantas que cultivé en siglos, desde el pie de las nieves hasta los
          bosques donde tienen sus guaridas los osos salvajes.
Curaré tu fatiga que a veces te nubla como bala de plomo; te recrearé con la luz de
          las cien flores de quinua, con la imagen de su danza al soplo de los vientos;
          con el pequeño corazón de la calandria en que se retrata el mundo; te refres-
          caré con el agua limpia que canta y que yo arranco de la pared de los
          abismos que tiemplan con su sombra a nuestras criaturas.
¿Trabajaré siglos de años y meses para que alguien que no me conoce y a quien no
          conozco me corte la cabeza con una maquina pequeña?

No, hermanito mio. No ayudes a afilar esa máquina contra mi; acércate, deja que
          te conozca; mira detenidamente mi rostro, mis venas; el viento que va de mi
          tierra a la tuya es el mismo; el mismo viento respiramos; la tierra en que tus
          máquinas, tus libros y tus flores cuentas, baja de la mia, mejorada, amansada.
Que afilen cuchillos, que hagan tronar zurriagos; que masen barro para desfugurar
          nuestros rostros; que todo eso hagan.
No tememos a la muerte; durante siglos hemos ahogado a la muerte con nuestra
          sangre, la hemos hecho danzar en caminos conocidos y no conocidos.
Sabemos que pretenden desfigurar nuestros rostros von barro; mostramos asi,
          desfigurados, ante nuestros hijos para que ellos nos maten.

No sabemos bien qué ha de suceder. Que camine la muerta hacia nosotros; que
          vengan esos hombres a quienes no conocemos. Los esperaremos en guardia;
          somos hijos del padre de todos los rios, del padre de todas las montanas.
          ¿Es que ya no vale nada el mundo, hermanito doctor?
No contestes que no vale. Más grande que mi fuerza en miles de años aprendida;
          que los músculos de me cuello en miles de meses, en miles de años fortaleci-
          dos, es la vida, la eterna vida mia, el mundo que no descansa, que crea sin
          fatiga; que pare y forma como el tiempo, sin fin y sin precipicio.

Marzo, 1966

[1] CUZCO *1979*

[2] CUZCO *1983*

[3] CUZCO *1988*

[4] LIMA *1988*

[5] WEDDING RECEPTION, CHINCHERO 1988

[6] CCOYU RITTI FESTIVAL, NEAR CUZCO *1988*

[7] PALM SUNDAY, CHINCHERO 1988

[8] WEDDING, CHINCHERO *1988*

[9] MATADORES, LIMA *1983*

[10] BROTHERS, LIMA *1983*

[11] CUZCO *1979*

[12] CUZCO *1981*

[13] LIMA *1983*

[14] CHINCHERO *1983*

[15] CHINCHERO *1983*

[16] CHINCHERO *1983*

[17] CUZCO *1988*

[18] WEDDING BAND, CHINCHERO *1988*

[19] CHINCHERO 1978

[20] CHINCHERO *1988*

[21] SHANTY TOWN, LIMA *1979*

[22] CHINCHERO *1981*

[23] LIMA *1979*

[24] SAN JUAN *1988*

[25] CHIMBOTE *1988*

[26] POTATO HARVEST, CHINCHERO *1987*

[27] **SHANTY TOWN, LIMA** *1987*

[28] SHANTY TOWN, LIMA *1987*

[30] POPE´S VISIT, LIMA *1988*

[31] CAJAMARCA *1989*

[32] CUZCO 1988

[33] CHINCHERO *1983*

[34] CHINCHERO *1981*

[35] URUBAMBA VALLEY *1988*

[36] CHINCHERO *1981*

[37] CHINCHERO *1983*

[39] CUZCO *1981*

[40] CHINCHERO *1983*

[41] BUS STOP, CHINCHERO *1987*

[42] WEDDING RECEPTION, CHINCHERO *1988*

[43] CHINCHERO, *1988*

[44] LAST RITES, LIMA *1983*

[45] SHANTY TOWN, LIMA *1983*

[46] CEMETERY, LIMA *1983*

[47] CHINCHERO *1988*

Acknowledgments

I am deeply grateful to the people of Peru for their generosity and patience, to my family and friends for their years of support and encouragement, and to Mark Bussell, Ronn Campisi, Deborah Cramer, Alice Rose George, Jeff Jacobson, Christine Graves, Father Michael and the Benedictine Fathers of Peru, the family of Dr. Oscar and Jean Miro Quesada, Kathy Ryan, Terry Reed, Eelco Wolf, Agfa Corporation and The Fulbright Commission in the United Sates and Peru.

A very special thanks to Alain Jullien, who edited this work from the very beginning; Billy Hare, for his friendship, wisdom and guidance; Abigail Heyman and The Picture Project for their involvement with every aspect of this book; Dewi Lewis of Cornerhouse Publications for not only believing in this book, but making it happen; and my wife Rebecca, for her support and understanding, and for living and breathing this work with me every step of the way.